here
vhere

ing and
-tröm

000001035571

It's midnight in New York!
Taxis are honking, children
are sleeping, and somewhere,
somewhere an owl is
hooting!

New York is a busy city in the U.S.A.
Look out for bright yellow taxis!

It's midnight in New York – but out there somewhere, it's dawn near Newcastle. Most people are still snoring, but the postman is out and about and the cows have already been milked.

Newcastle is a busy town in England,
but it is surrounded by farmland.

5

It's dawn near Newcastle – but out there somewhere it's lunchtime in Taipei. A dragon comes dancing down the street! Look! Three men are doing their exercises. Above the din they can hear a bird calling.

6

Dragon parties are held in cities all over Taiwan.

It's lunchtime in Taipei – but out there somewhere it's two in the morning in Brasilia. A little girl has woken up. There's a party going on! She peeps out at the crazy moths dancing around the candles.

Brasilia is a city in Brazil where carnivals and parties can go on all night.

It's two in the morning in Brasilia – but out there somewhere people in Moscow have already eaten breakfast. A car has broken down in the middle of the rush hour! Angry drivers are honk-honking their horns…

Russia has hot summers, but the winters are icy cold. Moscow is often covered in snow.

11

It's already after breakfast in Moscow
– but out there somewhere it's only
six o'clock in Amsterdam.
A boat chugs along the canal
as joggers come panting and steaming
along the path.

Amsterdam is in Holland—
from here tulips and other
flowers are delivered to
flower shops all over Europe.

13

It's six o'clock in Amsterdam –
but out there somewhere it's midday
near Guilin, in China. Bikes are whizzing
past the paddy fields where wild cranes
are catching frogs. The cranes are
whoop-whoop-whooping!

14

Paddy fields are fields full of water where rice plants grow.

It's midday near Guilin – but out there somewhere it's early afternoon in Tokyo. Electric signs flicker and pulse. People are buying hot dogs, personal stereos are playing tss ss tss…

Tokyo is a very modern city in Japan full of flickering electric signs.

17

It's early afternoon in Tokyo – but out there somewhere it's time for the morning shopping in Madras. The markets are bustling, crowds are pushing and shoving. Monkeys are stealing bread and fruit.

Indian cities like Madras have markets selling spices, sugary sweets and brightly coloured fabrics.

19

It's shopping time in Madras – but out there somewhere it's breakfast time near Cape Town and the sun is already heating up the roofs. Mums are waving and kissing goodbye. Children rush for the bus swinging their school bags.

Cape Town is a city on the tip of Africa. It's a good place to grow grapes and pineapples.

21

It's breakfast time near Cape Town – but out there somewhere it's mid-afternoon on the Gold Coast and "surf's up". In the blink of an eye three skateboarders flip by. Far out in the bay a group of dolphins do somersaults.

The Gold Coast is in Australia – a great place for swimming and surfing.

23

It's mid-afternoon on the Gold Coast –
but out there somewhere dusk is falling
near Easter Island. A yacht is bobbing
up and down. Mum and Dad are
drinking coffee while baby is asleep.
Far below them a whale starts to sing…

Easter Island is in the
middle of the Pacific Ocean.
Can you see the huge stone
faces in the background?
It's a mystery who carved them!

25

Dusk is falling near Easter Island, but it's dawn near Newcastle and lunchtime in Taipei. It's two in the morning in Brasilia and rush hour in Moscow. It's six o'clock in Amsterdam and midday near Guilin. It's early afternoon in Tokyo and shopping time in Madras. It's breakfast time near Cape Town and mid-afternoon on the Gold Coast…

And it's midnight in New York!

When it's midnight in New York it's all of these times all over the World!

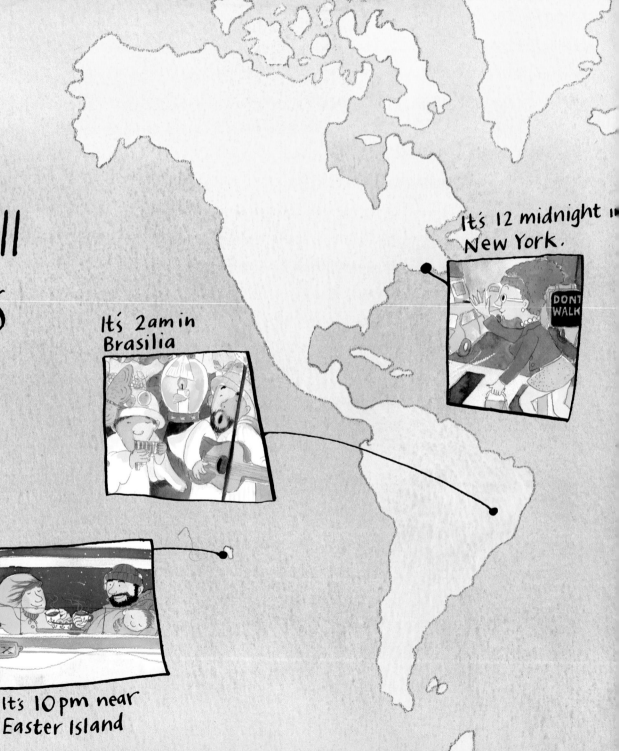

It's 12 midnight in New York.

It's 2am in Brasilia

It's 10pm near Easter Island

28

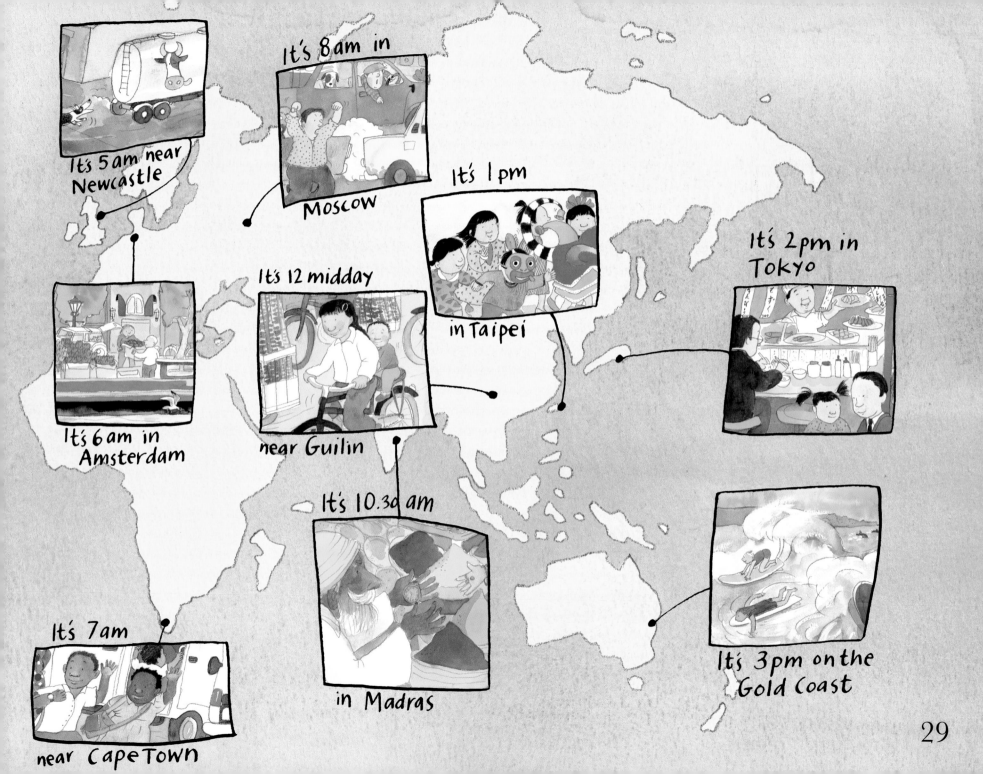

It's 5 am near Newcastle

It's 8 am in Moscow

It's 1 pm in Taipei

It's 2 pm in Tokyo

It's 6 am in Amsterdam

It's 12 midday near Guilin

It's 10.30 am in Madras

It's 3 pm on the Gold Coast

It's 7 am near Cape Town

29

As the Earth slowly spins one half of the world faces the sun and the other side is in darkness. That's why it's different times in different parts of the world.

Sun

When you are fast asleep in the middle of the night someone else far away is wide awake!

Helpful words

Days There are 24 hours in a day. A day starts from midnight.

Hours An hour is made up of sixty minutes and each minute is made up of sixty seconds.

pm and am All the hours after midnight are called *am* – 1am, 2am and so on until midday. After midday they are called *pm* – 1pm, 2pm and so on until midnight (see pages 28-29).

Time around the world In the past, different countries, and sometimes even cities, had their own system of time. A day could begin at lunchtime, or even sunset! The invention of trains changed all that. It became too complicated to catch a train when each place measured time in a different way. Over a hundred years ago a system of world time was introduced.

Time zones The world is divided into 24 time zones. It is as if lines have been drawn dividing up the world like segments of an orange. These are called timelines. The lines are not always straight, sometimes they curve around countries. This is because it would be too complicated if one part of a country was in a different time zone to the rest. But large countries like the USA are divided into a number of time zones. There is one hour difference as you travel from one time zone to the next.

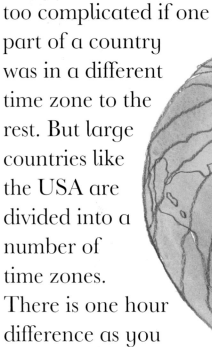

31

For Marit and Bosse

This edition 2014

First published by Franklin Watts,
338 Euston Road, London NW1 3BH

Franklin Watts Australia,
Level 17 / 207 Kent Street, Sydney NSW 2000

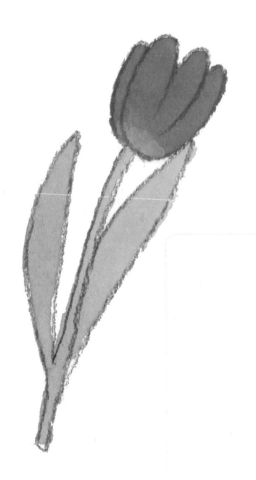

The illustrations in this book were made by Brita and Mick.
Find out more about Mick and Brita at www.mickandbrita.com

Series editor: Paula Borton
Art director: Robert Walster

A CIP catalogue record is available from the British Library.
Dewey Classification 910

Printed in China

ISBN 978 1 4451 2881 8

Franklin Watts is a division of Hachette Children's Books,
an Hachette UK company. www.hachette.co.uk